HOW DO YOU FIX A BAD DAY?

A CONVERSATION BOOK

WRITTEN BY
PAM CANTONE

ILLUSTRATED BY
KELSI CANTONE

Printed in the United States of America

Published in Hellertown, PA

Cover and interior design by Christina Gaugler

Illustrations by Kelsi Cantone

Photographs by Jaclyn Du Chateau Photography

Library of Congress Control Number 2021911786

ISBN 978-1-952481-29-1

2 4 6 8 10 9 7 5 3 1 paperback

For more information or to place bulk orders, contact the publisher at Jennifer@BrightCommunications.net.

Bright
COMMUNICATIONS

To my husband, Rob, and our daughters,
Kelsi and Casey:
Thank you for supporting and encouraging my dream.

This book is also dedicated to very important conversations
with so many friends and family. The words we chose to share
with one another make a difference. Thank you for inspiring me
to fix all my bad days.

How do you fix a bad day?

How do you make it right?

How do you find a good day,
when only the bad is in sight?

Timmy is having a really bad day.

He stayed up late and didn't go to bed.

He knew he'd be tired because that's what his mom said.

He missed the bus and was late for school.

He pushed a friend and broke a rule.

Now Timmy feels **sorry**
and really does **care**.

What do you think?
Would you like to share?

But first...

Let's take a breath.

Let's take a moment.

Let's take a look at what Timmy has chosen.

Let's begin with a breath
and a really good pause.

Then we can talk about
the "whys" and the "because."

**Pause 1 … 2 … 3 …
maybe a bit more?**

Pause again. This time maybe to 4?

1 ... 2 ... 3 ... 4 ...

Pause again. Yes, do it again!
Pause again and let's count to 10.

1 ... 2 ... 3 ... 4 ... 5 ... 6 ... 7 ... 8 ... 9 ... 10 ...

Now all is **calm** and not even a shout.

What is this day all about?

Maybe, just maybe, **we can talk it out.**

So, what do you think?

What do you say?

Is it possible? Could it be?

Timmy's having a good day?

Why do you think Timmy

What came
next?

What
started
this day?

How do you feel when
you are tired?

How do you think Timmy
feels when he pushes
his friend?

How do you think
Timmy's friend feels?

Do you think Timmy

night be having a bad day?

What was the first
thing that didn't
go right?

What if Timmy
went to bed like
his mom said?

What other good
choices could
Timmy make?

What can Timmy
do to fix this day
and make it right?

can have a good day?

Did you fix a really bad day?

Did you have a chance to make it alright?

Did you find a good day when only the bad was in sight?

**Because what you look for is what you find.
The key to a good day is a positive mind.**

Oh dear, oh my, not again.
Oh dear, oh my, Annie needs to pause for 10.

Annie is definitely having one of those days.

Milk was spilled and ruined her favorite dress.

She was mean to her brother, and her day's a big mess.

It just gets worse. Her day is just bad.

All she really wants is a hug from her dad.

Now, Annie feels **sorry**
and really does **care**.

What do you think?
Would you like to share?

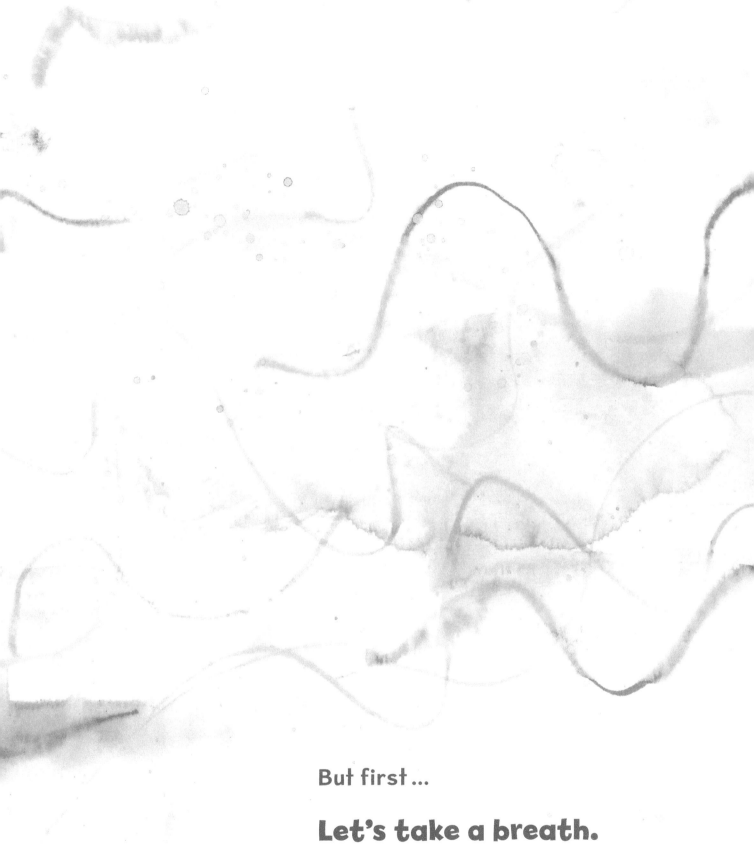

But first ...

Let's take a breath.

Let's take a moment.

**Let's take a look at what
Annie has chosen.**

Let's begin with a breath
and a really good pause.

Then we can talk about the
"whys" and the "because."

**Pause 1 ... 2 ... 3 ...
maybe a bit more?**

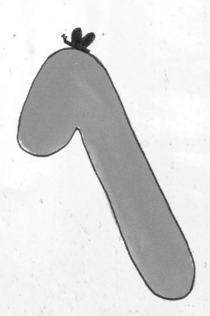

Pause again. This time maybe to 4?

1 ... 2 ... 3 ... 4 ...

Pause again. Yes, do it again!
Pause again and let's count to 10.

1 ... 2 ... 3 ... 4 ... 5 ... 6 ... 7 ... 8 ... 9 ... 10 ...

Now all is **calm** and not even a shout.

What is this day all about?

Maybe, just maybe, **we can talk it out.**

So, what do you think?

What do you say?

Is it possible? Could it be?

Annie's having a good day?

Why do you think Anni

What came next?

What started this day?

How do you feel when accidents happen?

What was the first thing that didn't go right?

How do you think Annie's brother feels when she is mean to him?

Do you think

might be having a bad day?

How do you think Annie feels when she wants a hug from her dad?

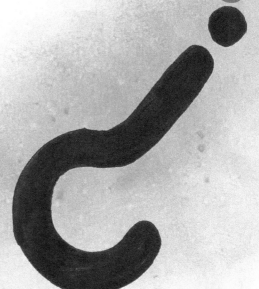

What can Annie do to fix this day and make it right?

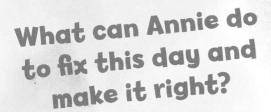

What if the milk didn't spill and ruin Annie's dress?

What other good choices could Annie make?

Annie can have a good day?

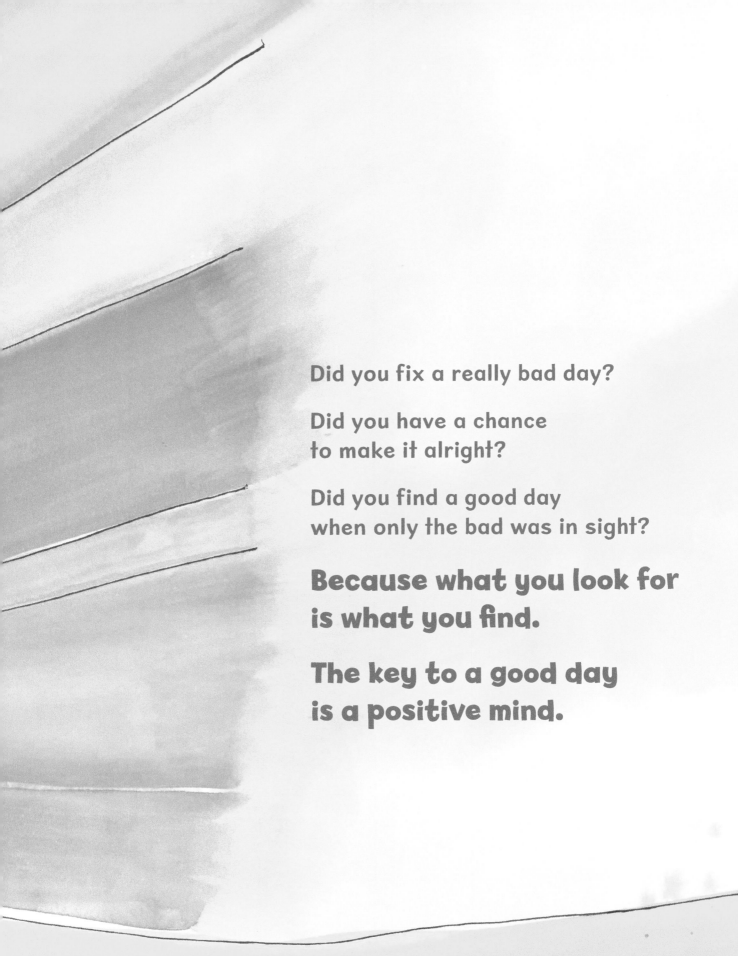

Did you fix a really bad day?

Did you have a chance
to make it alright?

Did you find a good day
when only the bad was in sight?

**Because what you look for
is what you find.**

**The key to a good day
is a positive mind.**

Uh oh, Peter is having a bad day and can't make it stop.

Let's start from the beginning. Let's start from the top.

Tumbling, tumbling, Peter fell
and scraped his knee.

Everyone laughed and laughed
and teased him, you see.

He's embarrassed and angry
and maybe a little sad.

He yells at his new friend
because he's so mad.

Now, Peter feels **sorry**
and really does **care**.

What do you think?
Would you like to share?

But first ...

Let's take a breath.

Let's take a moment.

Let's take a look at what
Peter has chosen.

Let's begin with a breath
and a really good pause.

Then we can talk about
the "whys" and the "because."

**Pause 1 ... 2 ... 3 ...
maybe a bit more?**

**Pause again.
This time maybe to 4?**

1 ... 2 ... 3 ... 4 ...

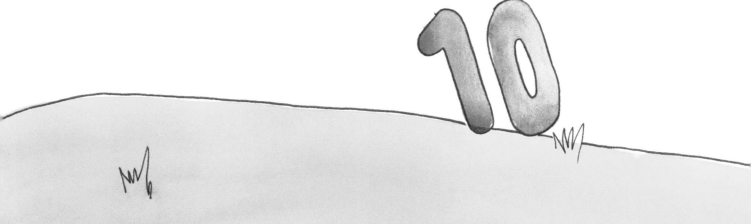

Pause again.
Yes, do it again!

Pause again and
let's count to 10.

1 ... 2 ... 3 ... 4 ... 5 ...
6 ... 7 ... 8 ... 9 ... 10 ...

Now all is **calm** and not even a shout.

What is this day all about?

Maybe, just maybe, **we can talk it out.**

So, what do you think?

What do you say?

Is it possible? Could it be?

Peter's having a good day?

Why do you think Pete

What started this day?

What cam next?

What was the first thing that didn't go right?

How do you feel when you fall or get hurt?

Do you think Pete

Why do you think Peter's friends laughed?

How could you be a good friend to Peter?

What other good choices could Peter make?

What can Peter do to fix this day and make it right?

...can have a good day?

Did you fix a really bad day?

Did you have a chance to make it alright?

Did you find a good day when only the bad was in sight?

Because what you look for is what you find.

The key to a good day is a positive mind.

Nothing was good, and nothing was right.

Our friends didn't have smiles shining bright.

But when we take a breath and take a good look,

Feel the feelings, pause, and maybe read a book,

We can make our day better. We can make it alright.

A good day is there. A good day's in sight.

And by the way,

Today WAS a good day.

**Because what we look for is what we find.
The key to a good day is a positive mind.**

The End

Dear Reader,

My intention for this book is to provide a moment to clear the mind, feel a few feelings, and see what you can find.

And the real beauty of the book is to unlock important conversations with children by using intentional questions as a guide.

Where the conversation goes is entirely up to you, the reader and listener.

May you take the time to **PAUSE** *and enjoy the moment to inspire* **A GOOD DAY.**

Stay Blessed,
Pam

Three Helpful Hints

- Allow the child to choose the direction of the conversation. Children have so much to say and want to share their wisdom. Let them be your guide.

- Select a few questions to start the conversation. You do not need to ask every question to have an important and meaningful conversation.

- Choose to focus on one character at a time. This approach respects a child's attention span and creates space to develop deep thoughts, feelings, and critical thinking skills.

More Conversation Starters

- Have you ever had a bad day?

- What can you tell me about a bad day?

- What feelings are the loudest on a bad day?

- What color would this feeling be?

- What would this feeling sound like?

- What would this feeling look like?

- What would this feeling smell like?

- Why is this feeling important?

- What can you learn from this feeling?

- What are good choices when we feel this way?

- Now, how can you find a good day?

For more helpful hints and ideas go to www.intentionalsoul.net or email the author at pam@intentionalsoul.net.

"What a wonderful addition to any classroom library! Whether this book is read silently or as a read-aloud, it encourages its audience to connect with the characters and offers a useful approach to diffuse a bad day."

—Mary Stauffer, former elementary teacher, Pinehurst, NC

"With *How Do You Fix a Bad Day?* Pam and Kelsi Cantone have created a vehicle through which parents and teachers can give children permission to safely express and experience their emotions. Pam's creative scenarios and questions, combined with Kelsi's charming illustrations, open the door to important conversations children need to have with the influential adults in their lives. This book is a useful tool for anyone living or working with young children."

—Adrian Kalikow, MEd, PCI Certified Parent Coach®

"The Cantones have written a book that uses an innovative approach to helping children stop and reflect on their feelings. Approaching the child through dialogue rather than commands to "Stop it!" is surely going to help prevent parents from going down the path of escalating emotions. *How Do You Fix a Bad Day?* teaches both child and parent to experience and examine feelings without reflexively reacting to them."

—Kevin T. Kalikow, MD, child psychiatrist
and author of *Your Child in the Balance* and *Kids on Meds*

"This book is a must for your collection. It has given my children (and myself) tools to help foster good conversations and to help handle tough situations and emotions. We all have bad days, but they don't need to stay that way!"

—Shawna Hoffman, parent, Macungie, PA

"You will want this book in your home to read to your children, your grandchildren, or even yourself. We all have bad days, but we choose how we respond to them, and that is exactly what this book, lovingly written by my friend Pam illustrates. *How Do You Fix a Bad Day?* gives structure to helping young minds-and yes adults, too-the ability to walk through how we can access our emotions in a constructive way and open a conversation to find healing and forward motion. By asking questions, we validate feelings instead of pushing them down, and that is exactly what can build healthy responses to hard situations. The bright and clever illustrations make it a joy to read and will keep even the youngest readers engaged."

—Susan Heid, creator and founder of The Confident Mom, PCI Certified Parent Coach®, and Certified Family Manager Coach®

"This book is a great conversation starter for the parent/grandparent that doesn't know what questions to ask. It lets children know that it's okay to not be okay all the time and empowers them to take control of their emotions. I can't wait to read it with my granddaughters!"

—Barb P., parent, grandparent, and educator

"This is a perfect book for future teachers to use to learn how to be comfortable with navigating the tough conversations about emotions they are bound to have with students. The best way to fix a bad day is to know how to talk through it."

—Hannah Skalski, pre-service teacher, Starkville, MS

About the Author

Pam Cantone is an early childhood and elementary educator, PCI Certified Parent Coach®, and Divine Sleep® Yoga Nidra Certified Guide. She is passionate about encouraging others to find the wisdom that is woven within life. Her family and friends motivated her to chase her dream to write a children's book that inspires conversations to find important answers from important questions.

Pam lives in Allentown, Pennsylvania, with her husband, Rob, and she loves to take walks with her rescued furry pal, Josie, or sit quietly with a cup of coffee to gather her thoughts. Her two grown daughters, Kelsi and Casey, and grandson, James, helped her become the mom, "GiGi," and author she is today.

About the Illustrator

Kelsi Cantone lives in Pennsylvania with her husband, Anthony, and is the new mom to her son, James. When she is not working full-time at her family's business or in "mom-mode," she finds joy in reading, drawing, and painting. She hopes to inspire the same love for books, art, and music in her children and others. She is thankful for the opportunity to collaborate with her mom on this book.

CPSIA information can be obtained
at www.ICGtesting.com
Printed in the USA
BVHW020347051221
623047BV00002B/10